THE TORONTO MAPLE LEAFS

ANDREW LUKE

Published by The Child's World®
800-599-READ • www.childsworld.com

Copyright © 2026 by The Child's World®
All rights reserved. No part of this book may be reproduced or utilized in any form or by any means without written permission from the publisher.

Photography Credits
Cover: ©Claus Anderson/Getty Images; multiple pages: ©Hanna Siamashka/iStock/Getty Images; GLYPHstock/iStock/Getty Images; md tauhidul/Shutterstock; page 5: ©Kevin Sousa/NHLI/Getty Images; page 6: ©Bruce Bennett Studios via Getty Images Studios/Getty Images; page 9: ©Kevin Sousa/NHLI/Getty Images; page 10: ©Matthew Tsang/Icon Sportswire/Getty Images; page 12: ©Matthew Tsang/Icon Sportswire/Getty Images; page 12: ©Andrew Mordzynski/Icon Sportswire/Getty Images; page 13: ©Dave Sandford/NHLI/Getty Images; page 13: ©Monsieurdl/Wikimedia Commons; page 14: ©Mark Blinch/NHLI/Getty Images; page 16: ©Bob Olsen/Toronto Star/Getty Images; page 16: ©Focus on Sport/Getty Images; page 17: ©Focus on Sport/Getty Images; page 17: ©Greg Abel/Getty Images; page 18: ©Bob Olsen/Toronto Start/Getty Images; page 18: ©AP Photo/Associated Pres; page 19: ©Ron Bull/Toronto Star/Getty Images; page 19: ©Steve Crandall/Getty Images: page 20: ©Claus Andersen/Getty Images; page 20: ©Mark Blinch/NHLI/Getty Images; page 21: ©Mark Blinch/NHLI/Getty Images; page 22: ©Claus Andersen/Getty Images; page 22: ©Graig Abel/Getty Images; page 25: ©Conn Smythe Fonds/Archives of Ontario/Wikimedia Commons; page 26: ©Bettmann/Getty Images; page 29: ©Scott Cunningham/NHLI/Getty Images

ISBN Information
9781503870697 (Reinforced Library Binding)
9781503871953 (Portable Document Format)
9781503873193 (Online Multi-user eBook)
9781503874435 (Electronic Publication)

LCCN
Library of Congress Control Number: 2024950387

Printed in the United States of America

ABOUT THE AUTHOR

Andrew Luke is a former journalist-turned-freelance writer. He has written about everything from chefs to China, but he focuses primarily on sports. Andrew is a lifelong fan of all sports, especially hockey. He lives in sunny Florida, where he enjoys spending time with his wife and kids.

CONTENTS

Go Maple Leafs! . . . 4
Becoming the Maple Leafs . . . 7
By the Numbers . . . 8
Game Night . . . 11
Uniforms . . . 12
Team Spirit . . . 15
Heroes of History . . . 16
Big Days . . . 18
Modern-Day Marvels . . . 20
The G.O.A.T. . . . 23
The Big Game . . . 24
Amazing Feats . . . 27
All-Time Best . . . 28

Glossary . . . 30
Fast Facts . . . 31
One Stride Further . . . 31
Find Out More . . . 32
Index . . . 32

Go Maple Leafs!

The hockey club we now know as the Toronto Maple Leafs came into existence in 1917 as the Toronto Arenas. They wore blue-and-white uniforms with a big "T" on the front. A few years and a couple of name changes later in 1927, the Maple Leafs were born. They now play in the National Hockey League's (NHL) Eastern Conference in the Atlantic **Division**. The Montreal Canadiens and Boston Bruins are their main division rivals. The Maple Leafs have 13 Stanley Cup championships, but they have not won the Cup since 1967!

Eastern Conference • Atlantic Division

Boston Bruins	**Detroit Red Wings**	**Montreal Canadiens**	**Tampa Bay Lightning**
Buffalo Sabres	**Florida Panthers**	**Ottawa Senators**	**Toronto Maple Leafs**

The Maple Leafs celebrate a victory over the St. Louis Blues during the 2024–2025 season.

Punch Imlach welcomes new players Andy Bathgate and Don McKenney to the Maple Leafs in 1964. Imlach coached the team for more than 10 seasons.

Becoming the Maple Leafs

The Toronto Arenas joined the NHL for its second season in 1918. In 1919, brothers Fred and Percy Hambly bought the team from the Toronto Arena Company and renamed it the Toronto St. Patricks. The St. Pats played in green-and-white uniforms. When Conn Smythe bought the team eight years later in 1927, he changed their colors back to blue and white.

Toronto has had two **dynasty** periods. Between 1947 and 1951, they won four Stanley Cups. Hall of Fame centers Syl Apps and Ted Kennedy were the captains of those teams. Then, from 1962 through 1967, center Dave Keon and the Leafs won four Cups in six years, including three straight from 1962 to 1964. Montreal is the only other NHL team to win at least three Cups in a row twice.

By the Numbers

The Maple Leafs are one of the league's most well-known teams. Here are some interesting numbers associated with the team:

13 — The Maple Leafs' 13 Stanley Cups are the second-most of all time. Only the Montreal Canadiens have more, with 24.

3 — Only three Toronto players have ever been named the NHL's Most Valuable Player (MVP): Ted Kennedy, Babe Pratt, and Auston Matthews.

10 — Maple Leafs star center Darryl Sittler holds the NHL record for most points in a single game, with 10.

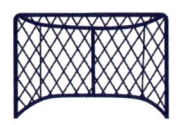

21 — George "Chief" Armstrong played all 21 of his NHL seasons in Toronto, the most of any Leafs player.

In just eight seasons, Auston Matthews established himself as the greatest player ever to play for the Maple Leafs. ▶

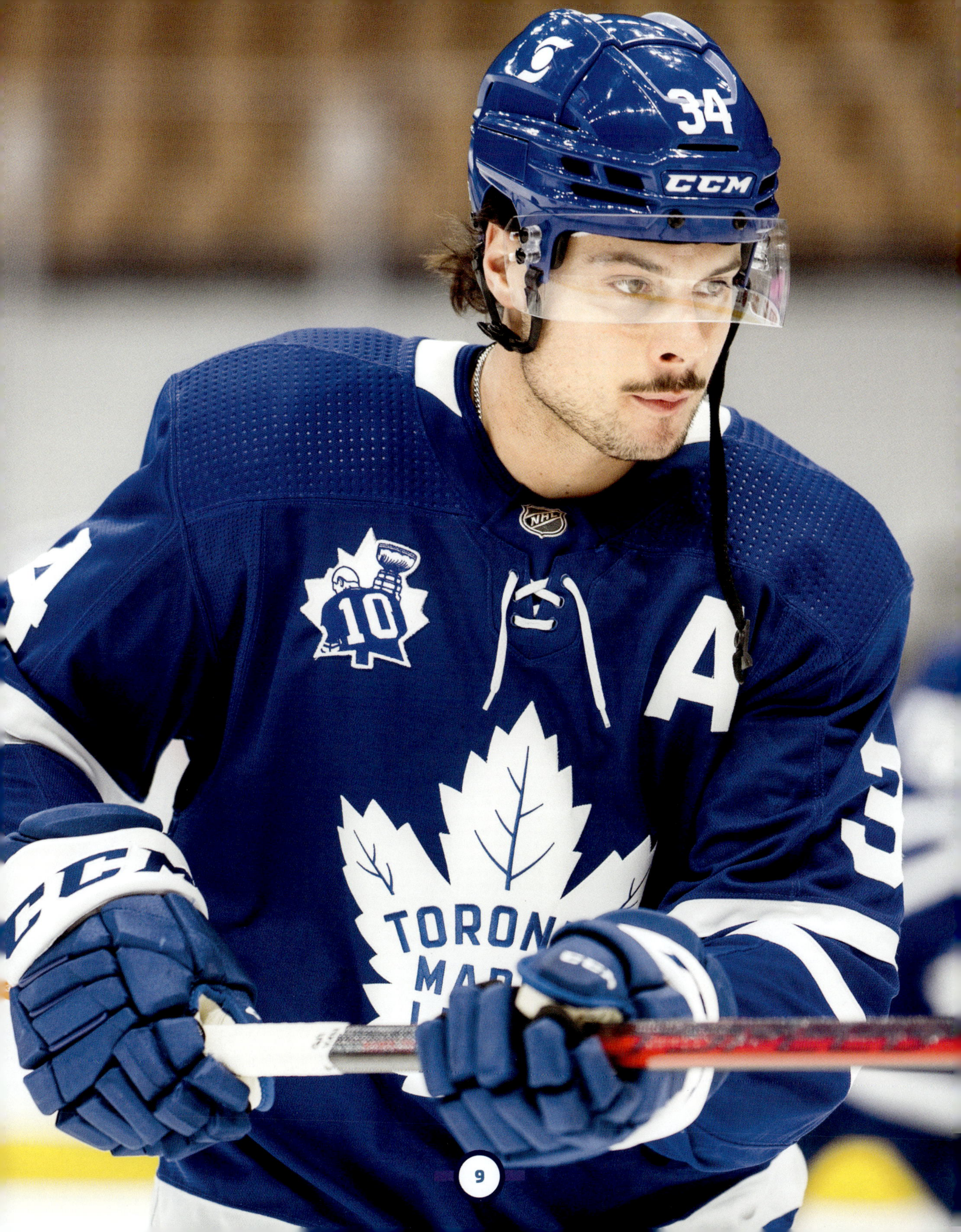
34
CCM
NHL
10
A
TORON

Scotiabank Arena is also home to the Toronto Raptors of the National Basketball Association (NBA).

Game Night

Since 1999, the Maple Leafs have called Scotiabank Arena home. The arena seats 18,800 hockey fans and is almost always sold out for Leafs games. The building replaced Maple Leaf Gardens as home to the Leafs. Maple Leaf Gardens was Toronto's home arena beginning in 1931. The Maple Leafs won 11 of their 13 Stanley Cups there. The building is still standing on the corner of Church and Carlton Streets in Toronto. The team's mascot is named Carlton after the location.

We're Famous!

When the Leafs are mentioned in popular culture, it's usually because a famous Canadian is involved. Pop star Justin Bieber often wears a Toronto jersey when he performs live. In 2008, comedian Mike Myers made the team the focus of his movie *The Love Guru*. In the film, Myers' character is a self-help guru hired by the team to help them start winning games.

Uniforms

HOME

AWAY

Real-Life Cujo

Curtis Joseph was the Maple Leafs' starting goaltender from 1998 until 2002. During his first season with the Leafs, he revealed his mask design. It featured an image of a mad, snarling dog with a wide open mouth. Joseph had the word "Cujo" painted on the side of the mask. Cujo was Joseph's nickname, made up of the first two letters of his first and last names. Cujo was also the title character of a 1981 horror novel about a rabid dog by famous author Stephen King.

Truly Weird

People often comment that the name Maple Leafs is grammatically incorrect. After all, the plural of *leaf* is *leaves*. But the word *Leafs* is not about the things that grow on trees. Instead, the reference is to the Maple Leaf, a badge worn by a group of Canadian soldiers in World War I. Since Maple Leaf is a proper noun, you just add an "s" to make it plural. New owner Conn Smythe changed the team's name from the St. Patricks to the Maple Leafs in 1927. That's when the team began wearing the familiar big blue leaf on the front of their uniforms.

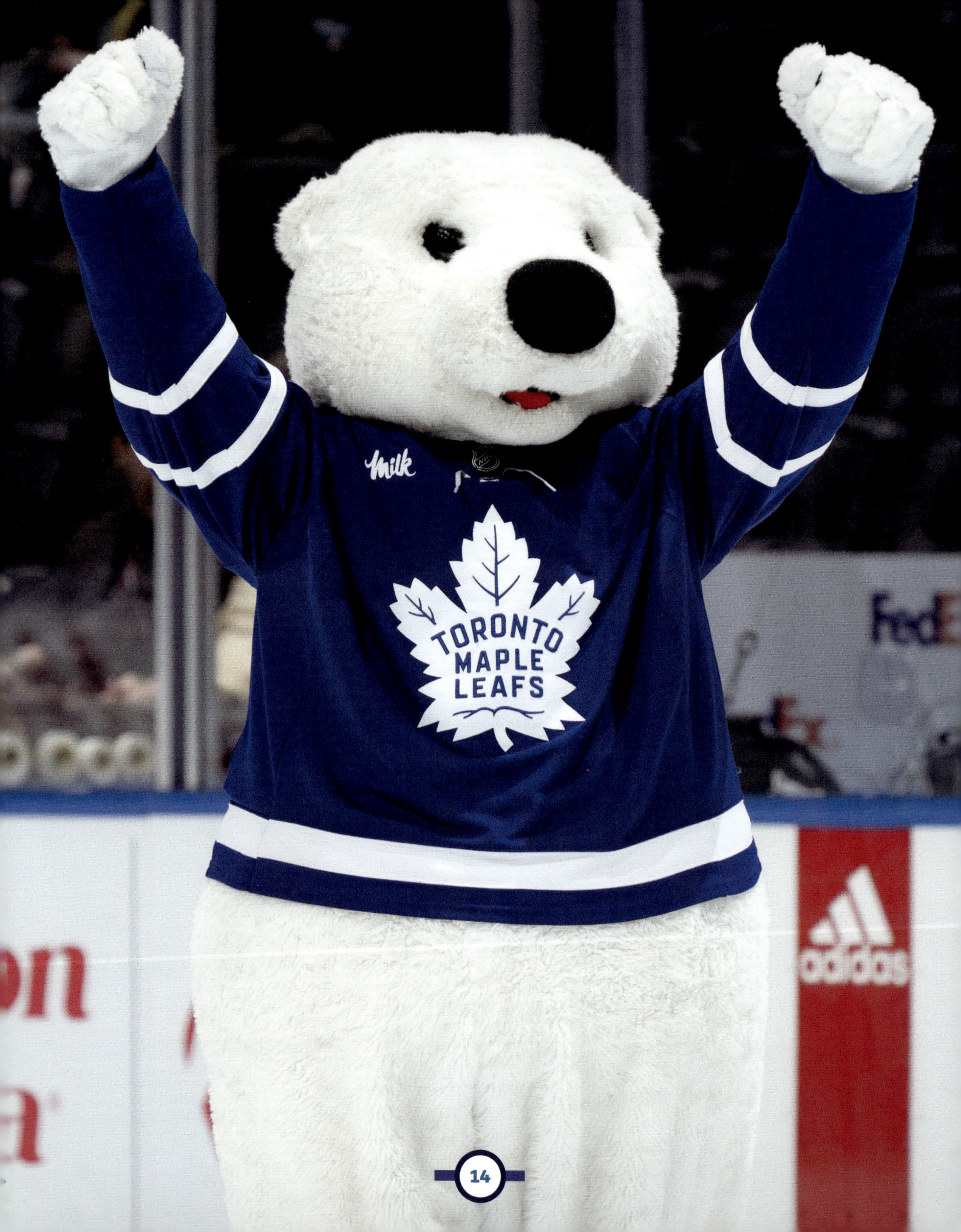
Milk
TORONTO
MAPLE
LEAFS
adidas

Team Spirit

The Maple Leafs' mascot is a giant white polar bear named Carlton. He is named in honor of the street location of Maple Leaf Gardens, the arena where the Leafs played for 68 years. Carlton wears a Leafs jersey with the number 60 for 60 Carlton Street. Carlton was created in 1995. The Leafs were trying to attract new fans. After many losing seasons, the team was looking for a way to connect with new, younger fans. Now, the seats in the arena are always full. Carlton is a popular fixture at Scotiabank Arena, entertaining and revving up fans before and during games.

◀ When he isn't cheering for the Maple Leafs at Scotiabank Arena, Carlton is making appearances around the Toronto area and posing for Instagram posts.

Heroes of History

Dave Keon
Center | 1960–1975

Twenty-year-old Dave Keon made quite an impression during his **rookie** season in 1960. Keon scored 20 goals and earned 45 points to win the Calder Trophy as NHL Rookie of the Year. He went on to be one of the all-time Leafs leaders in goals, assists, and points. Keon was part of the Leafs dynasty that won four Stanley Cups in the 1960s. He was named captain of the Leafs in 1969 and became part of the Hockey Hall of Fame in 1986.

Börje Salming
Defenseman | 1973–1989

Börje Salming was an NHL **pioneer**. The Swedish superstar was the first European-trained player to make a big difference in the league. He was a tough defender, but he could also score big goals when needed. He scored 148 for the Maple Leafs! Salming was the first European player to play 1,000 NHL games. The six-time **All-Star** retired as the Leafs' career leader in goals, assists, and points by a defenseman.

Darryl Sittler
Center | 1970–1982

Darryl Sittler replaced Dave Keon as Maple Leaf captain in 1975. In his first season as captain, Sittler scored 100 points. This included a record 10-point game against Boston. Two seasons later, he had 117 points, which earned him a spot on the All-Star team. That was the best season of his Hall of Fame career. He scored 1,121 career points. Sittler was added to the Hockey Hall of Fame in 1989.

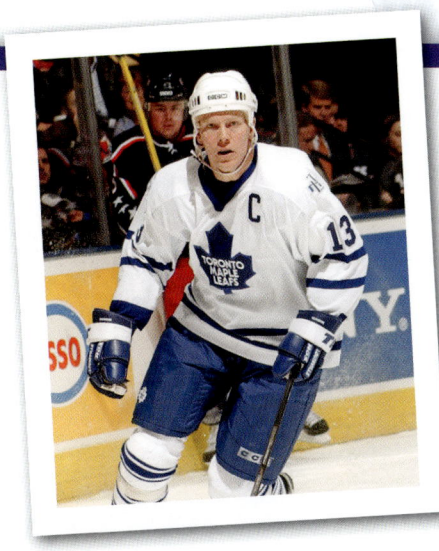

Mats Sundin
Center | 1994–2008

By the 1990s, it was common for Swedish players to follow the trail blazed by Börje Salming to play in the NHL. Mats Sundin had proven himself as a star player in the league when he was traded from Quebec to Toronto in 1994. The big Swede became a superstar in Toronto. He became team captain in 1997 and went on to play 13 total seasons in Toronto. Sundin retired as the Maple Leafs' all-time leader in goals, with 420, and points, with 987.

Big Days

NOVEMBER 12, 1931

The Maple Leafs' brand-new arena, Maple Leaf Gardens, opens with a game against the Chicago Blackhawks. The game is the first of the season for both teams. The Blackhawks win 2–1.

Maple Leafs defenseman Bill Barilko's last career goal is a big one. He scores the Stanley Cup-winning goal in **overtime** of Game 5. Sadly, Barilko is killed in an accident after the season ends.

APRIL 21, 1951

FEBRUARY 7, 1976

Maple Leafs captain Darryl Sittler has the best game in NHL history. He scores a record 10 points against the Boston Bruins. This includes six goals and four assists.

Team captain Wendel Clark is traded to the Quebec Nordiques in a huge deal that brings future Hall of Famer Mats Sundin to Toronto. The trade of the highly popular Clark is a shocking move for Maple Leafs fans.

JUNE 28, 1994

Modern-Day Marvels

John Tavares
Center | 2018–Present

In 2009, the New York Islanders picked John Tavares first overall in the NHL **Draft**. He played nine successful seasons with the Islanders and served as the team's captain. Most people expected that Tavares would keep playing for the Islanders when his contract expired. Instead, the Islanders captain signed with his hometown Maple Leafs for the 2018–2019 season. In his first season with the Leafs, Tavares scored a career-high 47 goals. He was named the 18th captain in Maple Leafs history in 2019.

Mitch Marner
Right Wing | 2016–Present

Mitch Marner is constantly looking to set up his teammates for chances to score. He was the fourth overall pick in the 2015 NHL Draft. Marner made a difference for his new team right away. He earned 42 assists and 61 points as a rookie. This earned him a spot on the NHL All-Rookie team. The two-time All-Star scored 99 points in 2022–2023, including a career-high 69 assists.

William Nylander
Right Wing | 2015–Present

The Maple Leafs drafted Swedish winger William Nylander eighth overall in 2014. Nylander's father played 15 seasons in the NHL, so he grew up around NHL players. He is a smooth skater and gifted goal scorer. Nylander broke out in 2021–2022, scoring 80 points. He followed that up with back-to-back 40-goal seasons. Thanks to his work on the ice, the Maple Leafs agreed to pay Nylander $92 million to stay with the team until 2031.

Morgan Rielly
Defenseman | 2013–Present

Morgan Rielly has been a dependable part of the Maple Leaf defense for more than 10 years. The Leafs picked Rielly fifth overall in the 2012 NHL Draft, and he quickly became a difference-maker for the team. Rielly is an offensively minded defenseman—even when he is stopping the other team from scoring, he is thinking of ways to help his team score. This was on display during the 2018–2019 season. That year, Rielly scored a career-high 20 goals. He followed this up with a career-high 58 assists in 2021–2022.

Auston Matthews has led the NHL in several single-season stat categories, including hat tricks, shots on goal, and goals per game across his first eight seasons with the Maple Leafs.

The G.O.A.T.

Auston Matthews was the number one pick in the 2016 NHL Draft and was named the NHL Rookie of the Year. In 2023–2024, he set the Leafs' record for goals scored in a single season with 69. He has led the NHL in single-season goals three times and is just the ninth player in NHL history to score at least 60 goals in multiple seasons. The five-time All-Star ranks fifth in NHL history in career goals scored per game. With many more seasons of playing in his future, Matthews will continue breaking NHL records for years to come.

Fan Favorite

Wendel Clark was beloved by Leafs fans because of his style of play. The former Toronto captain was a very physical hockey player. He was always willing to stand up for a teammate when needed. Clark was also a great goal scorer. He ranks in the top 10 in all-time Leafs goals scored.

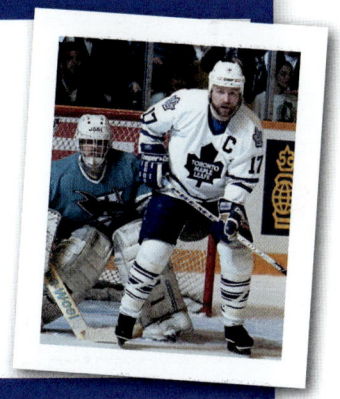

The Big Game

It is hard for a hockey team to win in the **playoffs** when they lose the first three games in the series. That means the team has to win four games in a row to move on in the playoffs. It is rare for a team to manage this feat. It has only ever happened five times in American professional sports—once in Major League Baseball and four times in the NHL. The Maple Leafs were the first to do it. After losing the first three games to the Detroit Red Wings, they won Games 4, 5 and 6 of the 1942 Stanley Cup Final. Then, tied three games to three, the Maple Leafs won Game 7 to complete their comeback. Detroit scored first and held a 1-0 lead to start the third period, but the Leafs scored three times in the final period to claim the Stanley Cup victory. It was the first Stanley Cup Final where all seven games were played, and the fourth championship for Toronto.

The Maple Leafs celebrate their amazing comeback in the 1942 Stanley Cup Final. ▶

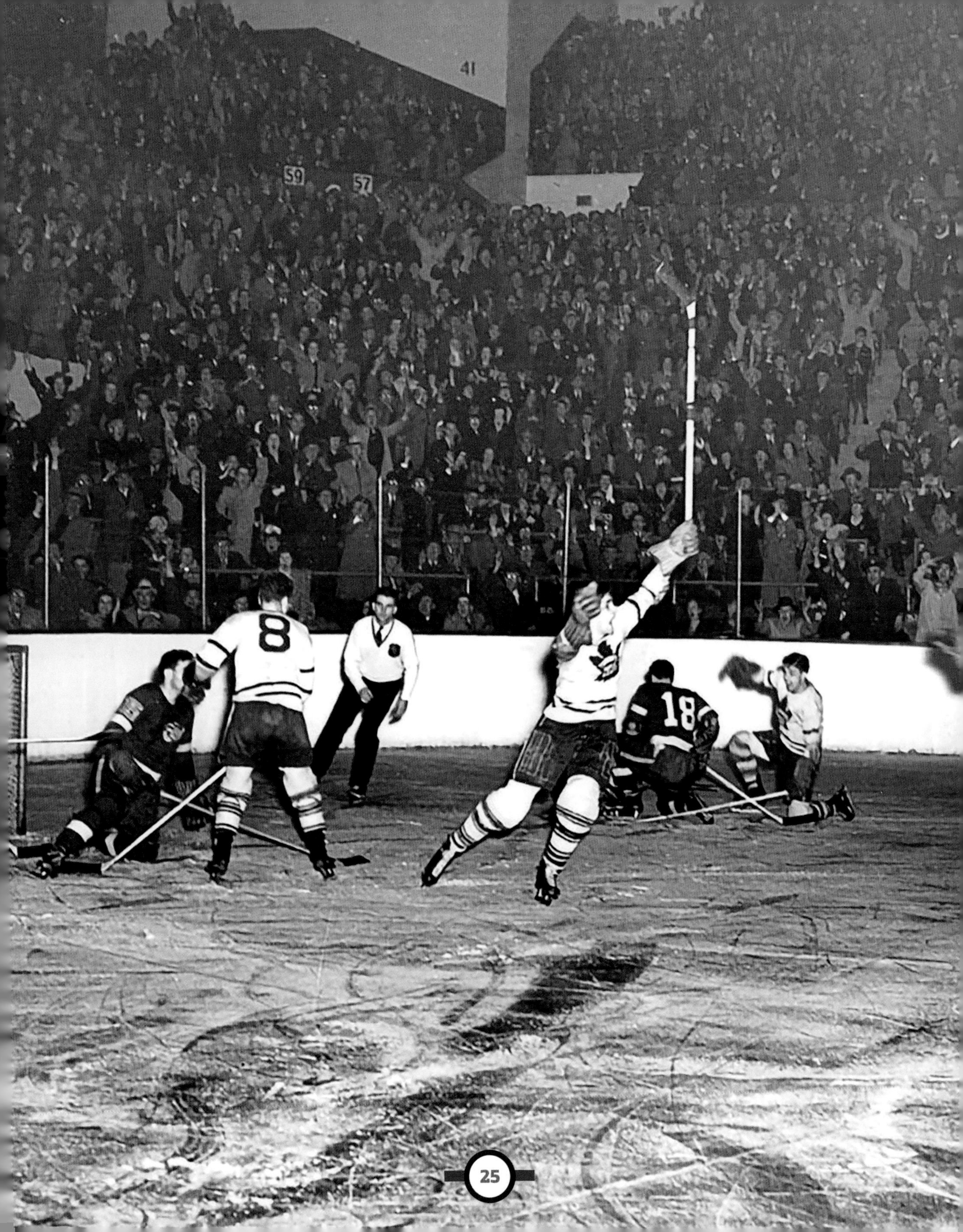
41
59
57
8
18

Maple Leafs goalie Harry Lumley fights a Detroit Red Wings player for the puck in a 1954 game.

Amazing Feats

Shutouts
In 1953–1954, Maple Leafs goalie Harry Lumley posted 13 shutouts to break his own record of 10 shutouts from the season before.

13

Goals
Maple Leafs superstar center Auston Matthews scored a team record 69 goals in 2023–2024. This broke his own record of 60 goals set in 2021–2022.

69

Assists
Former Leafs captain Doug Gilmour passed out 95 assists in 1992–1993. This broke the previous Leafs season record by more than 20 assists.

95

Power Play Goals
Wendel Clark and Dave Andreychuk share the team record for **power play** goals scored in a season, with 21 each in 1993–1994.

21

All-Time Best

MOST POINTS
1	Mats Sundin	987
2	Darryl Sittler	916
3	Dave Keon	858
4	Börje Salming	768
5	George Armstrong	713

MOST HAT TRICKS
1	Darryl Sittler	18
2	Babe Dye	16
3	Charlie Conacher	14
4	Auston Matthews*	13
5	Rick Vaive	10

MOST GOALS
1	Mats Sundin	420
2	Darryl Sittler	389
3	Auston Matthews*	378
4	Dave Keon	365
5	Ron Ellis	332

MOST WINS
1	Turk Broda	304
2	Johnny Bower	219
3	Felix Potvin	160
4	Frederik Andersen	149
5	Curtis Joseph	138

MOST ASSISTS
1	Börje Salming	620
2	Mats Sundin	567
3	Darryl Sittler	527
4	Dave Keon	493
5	Mitch Marner*	476

HIGHEST SAVE PERCENTAGE
1	Jacques Plante	.925
2	Johnny Bower	.922
3	Jack Campbell	.916
4	Jonathan Bernier	.915
5	Frederik Andersen	.914
	Bruce Gamble	.914
	James Reimer	.914

*stats accurate through December 2024

Mats Sundin celebrates a 2007 goal. Sundin finished his 18-year NHL career with 564 goals, 785 assists, and 1,349 points.

29

GLOSSARY

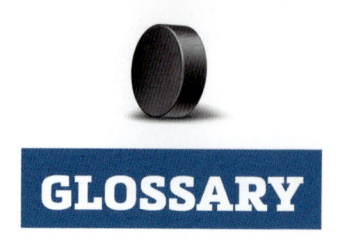

All-Star (ALL STAR) An All-Star is a player chosen as one of the best in their sport.

division (dih-VIZSH-un) A division is a group of teams within the NHL that compete with each other to have the best record each season and advance to the playoffs.

draft (DRAFT) A draft is a yearly event when teams take turns choosing new players. In the NHL, teams can select North American ice hockey players between the ages of 18 and 20 and international players between 18 and 21 to join the league.

dynasty (DIE-nuh-stee) A dynasty is a powerful group, such as a team, that leads or rules for a long period of time.

guru (GOO-roo) A guru is a person with special knowledge on a subject.

overtime (OH-vur-tym) Overtime is extra time added to the end of a game when the regular time is up and the score is tied.

pioneer (py-uh-NEER) A pioneer is a person or group that is the first to do something or go somewhere that has never been tried.

playoffs (PLAY-offs) Playoffs are games that take place after the end of the regular season to determine each year's championship team.

power play (POW-uhr PLAY) A power play occurs when a player gets a penalty and the other team has more players on the ice.

rookie (ROOK-ee) A rookie is a new or first-year player in a professional sport.

FAST FACTS

- Tim Horton was a Hall of Fame defenseman for the Leafs from 1949 to 1970. But he is best known as the cofounder of a popular chain of doughnut shops that share his name.

- Punch Imlach won 370 games over two stints as coach of the Maple Leafs.

- Nicknamed "Chief" in honor of his Native American heritage, George Armstrong played 1,188 games from 1949 to 1971.

- Tie Domi is the Maple Leafs' all-time leader in penalty minutes. He racked up 2,265 minutes over 12 seasons with the Leafs.

ONE STRIDE FURTHER

- Turk Broda and Johnny Bower are two of the best goaltenders in Maple Leafs history. They are the only goalies to play more than 400 games for the Leafs. Compare their careers and decide who you think was a better goalie.

- Compare the Stanley Cup to the Super Bowl, the World Series, and the NBA Championship. Which do you think is the hardest to win and why?

- The NHL's players come from a wide range of countries, from Canada to Sweden. Look up a list of the nationalities of all NHL players and rank the countries in order by how many players come from each one.

- Ask friends and family members to name their favorite sport to watch and their favorite sport to play. Keep track and make a graph to see which sports are the most popular in each category.

FIND OUT MORE

IN THE LIBRARY

Commito, Mike. *Leafs 365: Daily Stories from the Ice.* Toronto, ON: Dundurn Press, 2023.

Creamer, Chris and Todd Radom. *Fabric of the Game: The Stories Behind the NHL's Names, Logos, and Uniforms.* New York, NY: Skyhorse Publishing, 2020.

Laughlin, Kara L. *Hockey.* Parker, CO: The Child's World, 2024.

ON THE WEB

Visit our website for links about the Toronto Maple Leafs:

childsworld.com/links

Note to Parents, Caregivers, Teachers, and Librarians: We routinely verify our web links to make sure they are safe and active sites. So encourage your readers to check them out!

INDEX

Atlantic Division 4

Carlton the Bear 11, 15
Clark, Wendel 19, 23, 27

Imlach, Punch 6, 31

Joseph, Curtis 13, 28

Keon, Dave 7, 16–17, 28

Marner, Mitch 20, 28
Matthews, Auston 8, 22–23, 27–28

Nylander, William 21

Rielly, Morgan 21

Salming, Börje 16–17, 28
Scotiabank Arena 10–11, 15
Sittler, Darryl 8, 17, 19, 28
Stanley Cup 4, 7–8, 11, 16, 18, 24, 31
Sundin, Mats 17, 19, 28

Tavares, John 20